The Ham

The **Hampstead H**
long, connecting
Hampstead and th

No other part of sub._____ compares with its **Northern Heights** for variety of architectural heritage, parks and open spaces and associations with famous people. The Trail passes **500 points of interest** – one every fifty yards.

The Trail is divided into **five sections**. Each section starts and ends at a point easily reached by **public transport** and served by **pubs and cafés**. Though each section makes a good walk in its own right, sections can be **easily split** to create less demanding itineraries.

Hampstead has been a cradle of liberal opinion for over two hundred years. No other part of London has exercised such an attraction to thinkers, artists, reformers and campaigners.

Likewise no other transect of London illustrates so many different **styles of architecture**. The Trail passes London's most celebrated example of **Regency** town planning, many superb examples of late **Georgian** terraces and early Victorian **Italianate** villas as well as pockets of innovative **Social Housing** and **International Modernism**.

Hampstead Village has its own eclectic mixture of styles. Beyond Hampstead the route crosses **Hampstead Heath** and passes through one of the world's most influential examples of early 20th century town planning, Dame Henrietta Barnett and Sir Raymond Unwin's Arts and Crafts **Hampstead Garden Suburb**. The last section passes through London's finest surviving concentration of **Edwardian** domestic, retail and ecclesiastical architecture.

The five richly illustrated guides contain **detailed route maps**, a description of every **point of interest** along the route and information on the use of **public transport** to reach the start point and return from the end point of each section.

The route and its documentation have been devised by **The Highgate Society** in collaboration with the **Heath & Hampstead Society**, the **Hampstead Garden Suburb Trust** and the **Hornsey Historical Society**. The information was correct as of May 2012.

A companion trail to the **Hampstead Heritage Trail** is the five section **Northern Heights Circular Walk**. This takes in a further 350 points of interest along its nine mile route through **Highgate Village, Hampstead** and **Hampstead Heath**.

Reaching East Finchley

East Finchley is situated on the **High Barnet** branch of the Northern Line. From the West End or the City take a Northern Line train with the destinations High Barnet or **Mill Hill East** (not Edgware). Alternatively take a Northern Line train with the destination Edgware and change platforms at Camden Town. The start of the walk can also be reached by using the 102 bus from Brent Cross or Golders Green.

Journey time from Oxford Circus should be around 45 minutes.

Returning from Alexandra Palace

To return from Alexandra Palace to Central London take a W3 bus, destination Northumberland Park station, down the hill as far as **Wood Green** Underground station which is on the Piccadilly Line. Alternatively, to reach the Victoria Line, take a W3 bus in the other direction, destination **Finsbury Park** station. Buses run every six minutes on this route.

Points of interest: East Finchley to Fortis Green

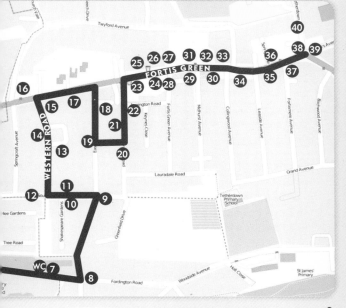

The requirement to accommodate trains from two different lines led to the **reconstruction** of the station in 1939 in contemporary style. Originally the electric trains used the outer tracks. Smoke deflectors projecting from the staff offices indicate that the inner tracks were once used by steam trains.

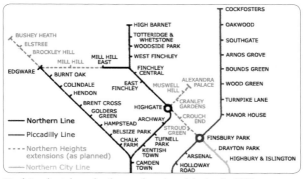

North London tube and rail network envisaged during the 1930s

In the 1930s the bold simplicity of its new stations placed London Underground at the forefront of modern architectural design. Along with Osterley and Arnos Grove, East Finchley is one of a number of stations whose commission, including interior fixtures and fittings such as up lighters and seating, was awarded to **Charles Holden** (1875 – 1960), the chief exponent of modernism on the underground. It is grade II listed.

Note the "**eye**" shaped glass panel in the windows. This used to bear the logo of the railway that owned the line, the LNER.

2 The red brick building on the far side of the station forecourt is the European Headquarters of **McDonald's**.

3 It and the station stand on what, before the construction through Hampstead Garden Suburb of Lyttelton Road and Falloden Way (see **D** 54), had been the Great North Road. This road used to be the principal coaching route between the City of London and the North. Travellers' needs were met by two coaching inns, the **Bald Faced Stag**, further up the hill, and the **Old White Lion**, just below the railway bridge, which had to be re-built in its present form to accommodate the construction of the Northern Line tracks in the 1930s.

4 Visible from the station entrance is the **Phoenix Cinema**. Opened in 1912, it is the second oldest continuously running cinema in the UK. It shows mainly arthouse films.

Until it became a park watercress was grown by the Mutton Brook, now in an underground culvert. Hornbeam trees were cut back every few years to provide wood for charcoal and oaks were allowed to grow to their full height for timber. Now that coppicing has ceased the hornbeams have grown tall and rangy and the wood has become more shaded. Wood anemones and other ancient plants can be found in the spring and nuthatch and great spotted woodpecker are often seen.

7 Past a children's playground and space for games is a café selling only **organic or natural food** beside a grassy picnic area. On the right side of the path are tennis courts and public toilets.

Café, Cherry Tree Wood

8 Continue along the path through ornate metal gates then turn left into **Indigo Walk**. Shortly on your right you pass houses built on land surplus to the needs of the grass covered reservoir you can see behind them. The spire beyond belongs to St James Church, Muswell Hill. Buckden Close further up contains single storey social housing intended for older people.

9 At the exit into Southern Road you unexpectedly find yourself in an enclave of mid Victorian villas. There are two villas immediately on your right, both grade II listed, and a well preserved row diagonally to your right. The latter owe their existence to the formation of the Harwell Park Estate which was laid out here on land acquired in 1852 by the **National Freehold Land Society**. This was established in 1849 by Sir Joshua Walmsley, **Richard Cobden** and **John Bright**, three Liberal Members of Parliament.

At that time only freehold owners were enfranchised to vote in parliamentary elections. By facilitating the acquisition of small plots of freehold land by people of average means, the object of the Society was to increase the number of adults **entitled to vote**. To this end in 1856 the founders formed the **British Land Company**, whose purpose was to purchase land and then resell it on the best terms to any customer who wanted to buy it.

12 At the junction with Western Road you can see two curiously isolated four storey town houses, almost Georgian in their proportions. These too are listed buildings though how they came to have been built here is still a mystery.

Turn into Western Road where you can see on your right an original **street name plaque**, unusually held to the wall with metal brackets. The fine series of villas on your left dates from the last decade of the 19th century. The iron railings of No 1 were recast from originals 'lost' in a front hedge when requisitioned for use for munitions in World War II. No 5 has plaster capitals with motifs typical of its time and a fine glazed front door. The roofs of the houses retain original pointed finials.

13 Look for the "VR" cipher on the **Victorian pillar box** on your right half way up the road indicating that it was erected during the reign of Queen Victoria. It stands outside Harwood House in which

Victorian pillar box: Western Road

both Oscar Wilde and Noel Coward once stayed.

14 The houses further up on your left are from **different periods**, No 17 dating from the 1880s, its neighbour, No 19, being built in 1925.

Harwell House: Western Road

15 The corner house on the right at the junction with Fortis Green has distinctive **barge boards** just below the eaves at the back and front.

16 "Westside", on the opposite side of Fortis Green, is a block of **"scissors" flats**, unusual in that each unit interlocks with the unit above or below, thus having an upper and lower floor. The development was a co-operative venture led by Colin

of a design common throughout turn of the century London. Note the high quality granite paving kerbs and the street gutters, still superbly preserved despite a hundred years' wear and tear.

21 The terraced houses on the far left of the street are separated by round arched passageways which provide access to their rear gardens via "**tunnel backs**", the name used in Hampstead Garden Suburb to describe passageways of this type.

Tunnel back: Lynmouth Road

The upper floor above these passages is divided between the two adjacent properties, one having an additional first floor room at the front of the house, the other an additional first floor room at the rear. This unusual arrangement of "**flying freeholds**" causes complications in deciding rights and costs when improvements or repairs are done.

22 On the right hand side of Lynmouth Road, on the side wall of the corner house in Annington Road, you can get a close view of a "**pebble dashed**" surface. Annington Road's houses were built after World War I when the inflated cost of building

Pebble dash: Lynmouth Road

materials restricted ornamentation to a minimum.

23 At the end of Lynmouth Road continue straight ahead along a pedestrian walk until you find yourself once again in **Fortis Green**. The gravel ridge you are now standing on was too acidic for productive farmland so that until the 19th century it remained common land used only for rough grazing. On your right Field Cottages, a terrace of four humble dwellings, were

11

Terrace are good examples of this practice. By 1900, as you will see when you reach Muswell Hill, parades of purpose built shops were incorporated by developers in the new suburbs that they built.

One of the shops belongs to **Leverton & Sons**, the seventh generation of a family firm of funeral directors founded in 1789. Their branch in Belsize Park is recorded at B6. They were appointed royal funeral directors in the mid-1990s. Look at the early photographs of Muswell Hill displayed in their shop window.

26 As with the naming of Lynmouth Road, how houses and streets are named provides an interesting commentary on changing social values. The date when much of Fortis Green was developed can be inferred from the use of Alma and Bomarsund, **battles in the Crimea War**, as house names hereabouts.

27 Next to Bomarsund is the **Alexandra** public house. The present building dates from the 1920s, before which time a beer house stood on half the site. Hidden away behind the pub are four of the last remaining back-to-back cottages in London.

28 Further along Fortis Green you come to a **police station** erected on the site of a former brewery. A plaque recording the date of its construction, 1904, can be seen just behind the blue lantern. The Police Station faces a terrace of **late Victorian cottages**.

29 Beyond Fortis Green Avenue is the **Emporium Tea Rooms** where by enjoying tea, coffee and traditional home made food on vintage bone china you can assist the work of Dimensions Community Enterprises who use the shop to provide training and support for people with learning disabilities.

30 Midhurst Terrace has two delightful small shops with curved frontages either side of the entrance to the flats above. Ceramic tiles with an attractive tulip design enhance the façade of the butcher's shop.

Micro retail units, Midhurst Parade

Centre, Twyford Court. This too was built by Collins. Note how the windows are framed by bricks of a different colour to the rest of the façade, a practice made popular by Lutyens in Hampstead Garden Suburb (see **C**77 and **C**84).

33 The Manor Health Centre, like Shakespeare Gardens, presents a forceful appearance of **Reproduction Tudor** with its black beams and white rendering. It was built as a showroom for the Electricity Company that was owned by Hornsey Borough Council before nationalisation.

34 On the right you come to Leaside Mansions, built by Collins in 1907. Look for the motif incorporating a **fireman's helmet**. There was once a fire station opposite.

35 **The Gables**, built in 1907 by Collins's

Emblem of firemen, Leaside Mansions: Fortis Green

sons, is an striking example of Arts and Crafts design with its imaginative use of iron balconies and protruding chimneys, its deeply recessed entrance arches and pretty windows of varied designs. Bays, gables, vertical tiling and chequerboard panels of contrasting red and yellow brick enliven the façade so that a frontage which could otherwise form a substantial mass is broken up into an assortment of pleasing elements.

The overall effect bears some resemblance to the twin entrance blocks at the gateway to Hampstead Garden Suburb at Temple Fortune (see **D**2) and contrasts with the sober uniformity of the later Collins blocks on the other side of Fortis Green.

The Gables: Fortis Green

both the upper and lower sashes created from small panes of glass. Contrast that with typical Edwardian window design illustrated below with the four small panes above two panes on the upper sash.

Neo-Georgian window, Woodside: Fortis Green

39 Built between 1897 and 1900 at the junction of Fortis Green, Fortis Green Road, Queen's Avenue and Tetherdown is a **Congregational church** now belonging to the United Reformed

Edwardian window, Muswell Hill Broadway

Church. Its architect P Morley Horder (1870 – 1944) is best known for his design of the School of Tropical Medicine and of the Trent Building at Nottingham University.

Prior to 1900 non conformist churches had often been situated in side streets. Muswell Hill has more than one example of the results of a more assertive policy to build these churches in **prominent positions**.

United Reformed Church: Tetherdown

This is one of four churches in Muswell Hill that are listed grade II.

40 Its church hall, built in 1928, is worth the short detour down Tetherdown. It is built in the **Jacobean** style, the pointed arches above the entrance door being relatively flat and having two different radii unlike doors and windows of the early Medieval period. It was designed by local architect Stanley Griffiths.

43 The colonnaded corner building, Queen's Mansions, was planned as a hotel but as a result of objections from the Congregationalists opposite converted to flats. Bear right beside a parade of shops into Fortis Green Road. This is one of a number of

Queen's Mansions: Fortis Green Road

parades of Edwardian shops in Muswell Hill, each shop being of uniform size and design. Their size is more convenient for **independent retailers** than multiple retailers who prefer to trade from larger premises. This has contributed to Muswell Hill retaining its attraction as a shopping centre.

44 Note the consistent design of the arches above each shop and the **decorative capitals** on the pillars beside the entrances to the doors from which the flats above each shop are accessed. This contrasts with the flats above the

Capitals on Queen's Parade: Fortis Green Road

parades built in the 1930s, (see **A** 97) which are accessed by a single set of doors.

45 On your right is what when it was built in 1925 was St James **church hall**, now a church centre for youth. Its architect, Grey Wornum, is best known for his design of the headquarters of the Royal Institute of British Architects in Portland Place. The building is grade II listed.

46 Further along is grade II listed **Birchwood Mansions**, built by Collins's sons in an Arts and Crafts style similar to that of The Gables in Fortis Green in the same year 1907. As with The Gables a potentially large and forbidding façade has been cleverly broken up into a domestic scale using both a

19

49 Note the care that Collins took when he designed **cross overs** at road junctions. Before roads were metalled they were muddy and dirty. Thus it was helpful, where a route crossed a side road, for pedestrians to be given protection by a cobbled surface. The stonework on this particular crossing is remarkably well preserved.

50 On the opposite side of Fortis Green Road from the New Century is the **John Baird**, a public house built in 1959 on a former bomb site. It is named after the pioneer of television who for a while worked at Alexandra Palace,

Cross over: Junction of Firs Avenue and Fortis Green Road

the BBC's first centre for television transmission.

John Baird (1888 – 1946) was a Scottish engineer who invented the world's first practical, publicly demonstrated **television system** and also the world's first fully electronic colour television tube. Although Baird's electromechanical system used at Alexandra Palace was eventually displaced by purely electronic systems, Baird's early successes demonstrating working television broadcasts and his colour and cinema television work earn him a prominent place in television's invention.

The time when Muswell Hill was built was a period of strong opposition to drinking, particularly among the two thirds of its population that were non-conformists. **Public houses** were not included in the new layout, as was the case in other new residential areas of that period such as Hampstead Garden Suburb (see **D** 56).

51 The small park on the opposite side of Princes Avenue from the John Baird was originally created to accommodate a large cedar tree in the garden of what, until it was demolished and the area re-developed, was **Fortis House**.

52 Cross Fortis Green Road keeping the John Baird on your right and walk down Princes Avenue. This, with Queen's Avenue, contains some of the **grandest houses** in Muswell Hill, some of

Enter the shop to see the wonderfully preserved fittings. Until very recently the shop retained the practice common in Edwardian times of having customers pay for their goods at a dedicated **payment kiosk** at the far end of the shop so as to keep the handling of money separate from the provision of service from behind the counter. This is the only shop in Muswell Hill listed grade II.

Note the representation of the business in the **mosaic** of small tiles at the entrance.

57 From Martyn's retrace your steps back along Muswell Hill Broadway and across Princes Avenue. The former Presbyterian Church is a remarkable creation in flint and a red North Welsh brick, particularly resistant to weathering. Its

Former Presbyterian Church: Muswell Hill Broadway

architect was George Baines. Listed grade II, the building was in danger of demolition in 1972 when the Presbyterians merged with the Congregationalists. In 1996 an imaginative scheme converted the church into a bar and dining area. Don't pass by without going inside.

58 From the entrance to the church you get a fine view across the road down **Hillfield Park** with its tumbling jumble of architectural features and its distant overview of the lower Lea and lower Thames valleys.

Hillfield Park

with a design which was more lavish than was usual for an Odeon and with unusual elegance and crispness. Part of an integrated development incorporating a parade of shops with flats above, Muswell Hill was the fifth and by general consent the finest of the Odeons George Coles designed.

Odeon Cinema foyer in 1936

Few other Odeon cinemas demonstrate so well the influence of German expressionism, a style adopted in Britain as a more sophisticated alternative to the historicist pastiches employed in cinemas of the late 1920s and early 1930s, and one more suited to the middle class clientele of Muswell Hill. Visit the interior if you can.

63 Use the pedestrian crossing from near Sainsbury's to the Odeon, then bear to your left. To your right is a parade of shops in a style typical of the 1930s. The contrast between the architecture on the two sides of Fortis Green Road, between the highly decorative Edwardian and the streamlined 1930s shops, is quite remarkable given that barely **a quarter of a century** separated these two developments.

64 Whilst admiring this difference take the opportunity to look at the detail on the **metal lamp posts**, reproductions of those of the period when Muswell Hill was being developed.

65 Across the road is the Anglican parish church of **St James** designed by J S Alder, a prolific church architect. This Grade II listed church was consecrated in 1902 and completed in 1910 with a 179 foot spire on a site 337 feet above sea level. It replaced an earlier church on the site deemed too small for the population of the growing suburb. This was a wise precaution as in 1903 as many as 650 worshippers would typically attend morning service in this church.

When **enemy action** destroyed much of this church in 1941 the congregation moved to the Athenaeum. They returned to a temporary building inside the ruined church in April 1944. The restored church was re-dedicated in 1952.

In 1873 a spur was created from a point between Highgate and East Finchley stations to provide access to Alexandra Palace. When it was still in operation it must have provided one of the most **scenic rail journeys** in London as it climbed London's Northern Heights through tunnels and over viaducts.

Until the development of Muswell Hill as a commuter suburb the line proved **unprofitable** due to the limited success of Alexandra Palace as a visitor destination and even after the development of Muswell Hill the line had difficulty competing with the combination of bus and underground as a method of reaching central London. Though consideration was given to its electrification after World War II, the line was closed to passenger traffic in 1954 and to goods traffic in 1956.

71 The section of its track between the former stations of Cranley Gardens, by Highgate Wood, and Muswell Hill was acquired by Haringey Council in order to create a **green walkway**. Sections either side of this walkway have been used as sites for primary schools and as a home for older people. According to an interpretation board 58 different bird species have been spotted on this section of the walk, blackbirds, robins and blue tits being the most common.

View of Canary Wharf and Shooters Hill from the railway viaduct

72 Shortly on your right, as the old track crosses a 17 arch brick viaduct, you obtain superb views towards the river Thames past Canary Wharf as far as Shooters Hill and the **North Downs**. On the north bank of the Thames you see the hills above Basildon in Essex and, further to your left, the woods of Epping Forest.

77 The grade II listed **library** on the left hand side of Queen's Avenue stands on the site of a former fire station. Visit the children's library on the first floor to view one of the earliest murals

Mural, Muswell Hill Library

in a public library, painted in 1938 by members of the Hornsey School of Art. It celebrates the founding of a chapel at the site of the well which gave its name to "Muswell".

The **diagonal metal bars** and panes of its windows are distinctively Art Deco as are carriage lamps and their supporting brackets. The Hornsey Borough arms and the construction date, 1931, are recorded in stone above the entrance doors. Compare the window detailing with that of the "eye" at East Finchley Underground station.

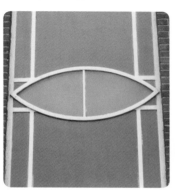

Art Deco window design, Muswell Hill Library

Art Deco window design, East Finchley Underground station

78 Previously located on the roundabout but more recently moved to a position on the opposite side of Queen's Avenue is a granite trough erected by the **Metropolitan Drinking Fountain and Cattle Trough Association**. The association was formed in 1859 to improve sanitary arrangements and to foster animal welfare. It was supported both by Queen Victoria's husband, **Prince Albert**, and by the **Archbishop of Canterbury** - celebrity endorsement was vital for a charity even then. By 1885 over 50,000 horses were drinking daily from the Association's troughs in London.

83 Few other streets in London offer such a profusion of different decorative features from the Edwardian period as **Duke's Avenue**. As in much of Hampstead Garden Suburb the unity and consistency of the overall building style is enhanced by subtle differences which differentiate each house or group of houses from its neighbours.

The houses on the left of the street are distinguished by their **pargetted gables**. The technical term for the painted designs is **sgraffiti**, whence graffiti. Note also the decorative ridge tiles on the roof and the distinctive flat roof above the bays on the ground floor. The photograph to the right illustrates a common feature of the Edwardian sash windows, the single pane of glass in the lower sash contrasting with the series of small glass panels that make up the upper sash.

Pargetting, 3 Duke's Avenue

84 Like many other corner houses in Duke's Avenue, No 11 incorporates a **polygonal corner section** which extends beyond the line of the front and the side elevation adding an interesting feature both to the façade

11 Duke's Avenue

and to the corner rooms inside. These corner rooms also provided the architects with challenges of how to roof them, resulting sometimes in towers sometimes in conical or polygonal turrets. Note the extreme complexity of the roof geometry of this house with its odd shaped attic rooms.

85 In common with other streets around the Northern Heights the decorative features of Duke's Avenue extend to the design of the garden walls, many of which make use of **mis-shapen bricks** arranged in the manner of crazy paving but often incorporated rounded arch-like patterns, as for instance surrounding the house at the corner with Wellfield Avenue. These are clinker blocks and end of clay clamps from local furnaces.

Numbers 31 and 33 are also distinctive for their flamboyant window designs.

88 A consistent feature of most of Muswell Hill is the white painted woodwork on the front of each house – the gables, the sash windows, the entrance door and its porch. Nos 60 - 68 are unusual in this respect in that their porches are manufactured from **cast iron**.

Decorative iron work: 62 Duke's Avenue

89 Whereas the front door of a Georgian or early Victorian house would be of solid wood, by Edwardian times the glazing as well as the carpentry of the front door would add status to the

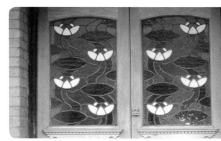
Non original glazing: 43 Duke's Avenue

house. Nos 37 – 51 all retain the highly ornamental pattern of glazing that originally decorated their front doors and the variety of different textures which allowed the light to reach the hall but at the same time protecting the privacy of the residents. On Nos 28 – 58 opposite you can see **decorative glasswork** in the side panels to the upstairs and ground floor bay windows.

90 The entrances to most front doors in Duke's Avenue are protected from the elements by a porch, often integrated into the design of the house. The **canopy** to the entrance of the corner house, No 90 Rosebery

Decorative porch canopy: 90 Rosebery Road

92 Now turn right along a path which leads under a railway bridge into **Alexandra Park**.

The bridge below which you pass once carried a direct, purpose-built railway link from the City via Highgate and Crouch Hill, which brought Victorian bank holidaymakers in their hundreds of thousands to a station incorporated into the new landmark of north London, the Alexandra Palace.

93 Spreading out in front of you is Alexandra Park, opened to the public in 1863.

Identity of Alexandra Palace and Park

Shortly to your left you will see the south west entrance to **Alexandra Palace**. Two visionaries, Owen Jones and anti-slavery campaigner Lord Brougham , recognising the critical and commercial success of South London's Crystal Palace, promoted plans for a rival "Palace of the People" and park to educate, exercise and amuse the newly literate masses of North London.

A company was set up and former farmland near Muswell Hill was acquired. At the top of the hill overlooking the park a huge **secular cathedral** was designed by John Johnson and Alfred Meeson. To create it materials were recycled from South

Entrance to Alexandra Palace

Kensington's International Exhibition building, designed by Captain Fowke, architect of the Albert Hall. The palace was opened in 1873 and named after Alexandra, the popular new Danish Princess of Wales who had married Prince Edward earlier that year. The palace complex incorporated a large nave, complete with splendid organ for concerts and exhibitions and with transepts leading to lecture halls, a theatre, refreshment rooms, art galleries and, at each end, a Palm Court. This combination of facilities made the Palace an ideal venue for

you can admire an equally **spectacular view** of Canary Wharf, the Olympic Park and beyond them Shooters Hill in South London, the second silhouette (B) on page 40. The terrace on which you are standing formed the southern limit of the last Ice Age. There is no higher ground between you and the Ural Mountains in Russia. You cannot see quite that far, but you can see over thirty miles on a clear day.

Looking back at the Great Hall, you can admire above the pedimented façade a **rose window**, as large as that of many cathedrals, set within a gable. There is a corresponding window at the north end. Originally caryatids flanked the doors. Still atop the roof soars a presiding deity, the Angel of Plenty.

Rose Window, Alexandra Palace

97 Continue your walk along the terrace until you come to the foot of a tall mast. From this point a fine view opens up of London's **Lea Valley**, the third silhouette (C) on page 40.

During the World War I the Palace and Park were requisitioned as an **internment camp** for German aliens, and the owners suffered financial losses. However a new invention was about to transform the Palace dramatically.

As you look along towards the east of the terrace look up at the bricked-in arcades. Behind them hides one of London's best kept secrets - two original **TV studios**, built experimentally inside the building by the BBC in 1935 when the Palace was chosen to inaugurate the world's first regular television service.

Original television mast, Alexandra Palace

The signal was transmitted by outside cable straight to the **300 foot high mast** specially built by Marconi. Its length had to be proportional to the radio wavelength and radiate in all directions. Because the foot of the mast is already 300 feet above London and has the uninterrupted line of sight for miles around necessary for short-wave TV signals, the antenna successfully beamed flickering but satisfactory pictures to the South-East's early televisions - and on a few occasions as far as New York!

section of the park. Around the lake are a few more statues to guard the "spirit" of the People's Palace - perhaps from further encroachment.

Boating Lake with "Leo the Lion"

From the stop by the car park a **W3** bus will take you to the Piccadilly line at Wood Green. The stop for the W3 in the opposite direction, which takes you to Finsbury Park Underground station, is located 50 yards to your right immediately in front of Alexandra Palace.

The View from the terrace of Alexandra Palace

The terrace of Alexandra Palace is arguably London's greatest viewpoint. Due to the vegetation in front of the terrace, this view is best enjoyed from three points, from the terrace outside the bar / restaurant, from below the rose window and from below the mast.

Crossness Recycling Plant, Belvedere (25 on map)

What you can see depends on the level of visibility, the time of day and level of intensity of sunlight. On a good day you can see as far as thirty miles. The map below lists the principal points of interest that you can see even on a day with moderate visibility. In addition to points of interest in the near foreground you should be able to see the towers of central

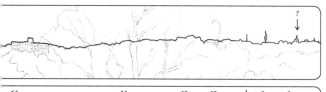

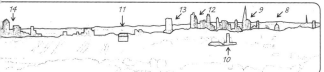

Vanessa Whinney

1 *St Michaels, Highgate*
2 *BT Tower*
3 *Millbank Tower*
4 *London Eye*
5 *Croydon Mast*
6 *Crystal Palace Transmitter*
7 *Strata, SE1*
8 *St Paul's Cathedral*
9 *The Shard*
10 *Hornsey Town Hall*
11 *Biggin Hill, North Downs*
12 *Gherkin and Tower 42*
13 *Bishopsgate*
14 *Canary Wharf*
15 *Shooters Hill*
16 *The Dome*
17 *Kingsdown, North Downs*
18 *Woodberry Down Estate*
19 *Olympic Tower*
20 *Olympic Stadium*
21 *Hornsey Parish Church*
22 *Woods above Belvedere*
23 *Littlebrook Power Station*
24 *Dartford Bridge*
25 *Crossness Recycling Plant*
26 *Pylons crossing the Thames*
27 *Tilbury Container Port*
28 *Pioneer Point, Ilford*
29 *Unite Building, Tottenham Hale*
30 *Walthamstow Flats*
31 *Laindon Hills, Basildon*
32 *Brentwood*
33 *Water Tower, Stapleford Abbots*
34 *Magistrates Court, Wood Green*
35 *Church, Buckhurst Hill*
36 *Spurs Stadium, White Hart Lane*
37 *Edmonton Incinerator*
38 *Flats, central Edmonton*

Further information

At **www.northernheights.eu** you can find out more about the Northern Heights Partnership, order other booklets and provide feedback.

More detailed information about Muswell Hill and Alexandra Palace can be found in:

Davies, Reg, Rails to the People's Palace, 1980

Gay, Ken, A Walk around Muswell Hill, 1987

Gay, Ken, Muswell Hill: History and Guide, 2002

Gay, Ken, Palace on the Hill, 3rd edition, 2005

© 2012 Hornsey Historical Society

Series Editor: The Highgate Society

Contributors: Keith Fawkes-Underwood, David Frith, Ken Gay, Jacob O'Callaghan, Janet Owen, Malcolm Stokes, Bill Tyler

Silhouettes: Vanessa Whinney

Publisher: Hornsey Historical Society

Distributor: Hornsey Historical Society

Designer: Nicholas Moll Design

Printer: Rainbow Print Wales

A CIP catalogue record for this book is available from the British Library.

ISBN: 978-0-905794-46-4